APOCALYPSE CAKES

RECIPES FOR THE END

SHANNON O'MALLEY

PHOTOGRAPHS BY KEITH WILSON

Running Press

PHILADELPHIA · LONDON

for **KATHLEEN O'MALLEY**

& KATHERINE ANANIA

On all of your birthdays

Library of Congress Control Number: 2010941097

ISBN 978-0-7624-4106-8

Cover and interior design by Amanda Richmond
Typography: Chronicle, Helvetica, and Cooper Black

Running Press Book Publishers
2300 Chestnut Street
Philadelphia, PA 19103-4371

Visit us on the web!
www.runningpresscooks.com
www.apocalypsecakes.com

ACKNOWLEDGEMENTS

THE FOLLOWING PEOPLE HELPED MAKE
Apocalypse Cakes **an unfortunate reality:**

Jean Sagendorph of Mansion Street Literary Agency
• Colleen Lindsay • Geoff Stone • Amanda Richmond
• Kate O'Malley • The O'Malley Family • The Wilson Family
• Tim Balon • Travis Matthews • Katie Anania • Dat Pham
Chelsea Weathers • Katie Geha • Sharif Youssef • Susan
Rebecca White • Alan Deutschman • PJ Raval • Kate Getty
• Jungshih Wang • Chris Barnard • Rich Heffernan
• Shannon Burke • Eric LaFleur • Kat Lam • Stephen, Julie,
and everyone at The Evolution Bureau •Russell Etchen and
Domy Books • Tim Corbett • Halley Bondy • Brooke Duthie
• David Groff • T. Cole Rachel • Kevin Lovelace
• Robi Polgar • Ayleen Perez-Marty • Brian Maschler
• William Blacklock • Alba Aragon • George Pasterk

CONTENTS

INTRODUCTION

WE'RE DOOMED. EAT CAKE.

A VARIETY OF CATACLYSMIC PUNISHMENTS
from God continue to rain down upon us.
Obviously, this is the time to eat several entire cakes.
Use this book to help you celebrate your time on this earth,
for when you look up from your cake-smeared cakehole,
the sky will fade ablack, the lakes will blaze aflame, and the
locusts will buzz aswarming. Eat now, little heathens:
there are no cakes in the apocalypse.

RAINING BLOOD
RED VELVET CAKE

THE BIBLE SAYS THAT WHEN THE WORLD GOES to shit, blood will rain down and fill our Six Flags slides with summer fun and excitement. Blood rivers will flow down flooded sub-development streets, sending Hummers awash over strip malls. Indeed, as Slayer reminds us in the band's 1986 song, "Raining Blood," the sky is turning red and the return to power draws near. What Slayer is trying to say in this verse is that basically we are fucked. What better way to prep for blood rain than eating a Raining Blood Red Velvet Cake?

RAINING BLOOD RED VELVET CAKE

CAKE

$1/2$ cup vegetable
  shortening

$1^1/2$ cups sugar

2 eggs

2 tablespoons
  unsweetened cocoa
  powder

Red food coloring

1 teaspoon salt

$2^1/2$ cups all-purpose flour

1 teaspoon vanilla extract

1 cup buttermilk

1 teaspoon baking soda

1 tablespoon white vinegar

FROSTING

1 pound cream cheese,
  softened

4 cups confectioners' sugar

$1/2$ pound (2 sticks) unsalted
  butter, softened

1 teaspoon vanilla extract

FOR THE CAKE, preheat oven to 350°F. Cream shortening and then beat in sugar gradually. Add eggs one at a time, beating well after each addition. Mix cocoa and food coloring, then add to creamed mixture. Mix salt, flour, and vanilla and add alternately with buttermilk, beating after each addition. Sprinkle soda over vinegar, pour vinegar over batter. Stir until thoroughly mixed. Bake in two 8-inch square pans for 30 minutes. Let cool to room temperature.

FOR THE FROSTING, put the ingredients in a bowl and cream with a spoon. Smear frosting on cake. In a separate bowl, mix $3/4$ cup of water with blood (or the bottle of red food coloring), find an umbrella, and splatter red mixture on cake with glee.

BLOOD RAIN *and the* APOCALYPSE

THE BIBLE PROVIDES US WITH ENTHUSIASTIC
accounts from people who thought that God cared about them.
In one famous ancient tale, God becomes enraged about something
and inflicts ten plagues upon the Egyptians, the first of which entails
rivers turning to blood. How exciting! Obviously, this blood had to come
from previously unseen blood-filled clouds whose contents God was
waiting to inflict upon the earth. So anyway, what it means for blood to
rain down on us is that God is mad again and wants to destroy us.

SEISMIC HAITIAN MUD CAKE

WITH ALL THE BATHROOM-BUGGERING POLITICIANS crushing already starved countries with embargoes, military interventions, and corrupt aid distributions, your nation is surely next to become so destitute that all you have to eat are cakes made of mud. Fortunately, we've developed a tastier version of this type of dessert for your pre-poverty palate. In fact, you'll relish its flavor for as many years as it will take for anyone to notice that you've been eating dirt for decades. So celebrate life now and try one of these organic Seismic Haitian Mud Cakes before the "First World" uses its foreign policy to starve you in the name of democracy, privatization, SUVs and Viagra.® You never know how long it will take for a disaster to strike that will guilt the international community into finally bringing you a meal.

SEISMIC HAITIAN MUD CAKE

5 pounds dirt
1 cup vegetable shortening
3 tablespoons salt

PUT YOUR DIRT into a strainer (or whatever's available) and hold it over a pot. Then run water (or whatever's available) through the strainer to extract the rocks, etc. Mix in the shortening and the salt. Then pat the mixture into a cake and leave it to dry under the scorching sun. The cake will be ready to eat after 12 hours, after which time you can decorate it with whatever happens to be around.

THE HAITIAN EARTHQUAKE *and the* APOCALYPSE

HAITI WON ITS INDEPENDENCE FROM FRANCE IN 1804 AND HAS literally been paying for it ever since. In 1825, France extorted the equivalent of $21 billion from Haiti in exchange for the island's freedom. France claimed that this sum was "compensation" for having lost the slave colony. Haiti paid its "bill" until 1947 (122 years) and has since endured so much debt, corruption, and manipulation by richer nations that it remains the poorest state in the Americas—so poor that they actually do eat cakes made of mud. In 2010, an earthquake struck Haiti and images of the country's centuries-long poverty were instantly broadcast throughout the developed world. All of a sudden, rich people everywhere flew to Haiti and got to be a part of something.

HAIL THE
DEVIL'S FOOD CAKE

EVERYWHERE YOU GO THERE'S A SATANIC orgy happening—on the corner, in the grocery store, at the elementary school. In fact, our age is so corrupt that there's probably a virgin sacrifice going on right now down at your local Laundromat on top of the soap machine. Better dance around in your underwear to death metal and try this sinful Hail the Devil's Food Cake before the junior-high kids hold another black mass and convince Lucifer to bring his sizzling hot gay minion dance party to your house.

HAIL THE DEVIL'S FOOD CAKE

FROSTING

15 ounces semi-sweet
  chocolate, finely chopped

$1^{1}/_{2}$ cups heavy cream

CAKE

2 cups all-purpose flour

$1^{1}/_{2}$ teaspoons baking soda

$^{3}/_{4}$ teaspoon baking powder

$^{3}/_{4}$ teaspoon salt

12 tablespoons ($1^{1}/_{2}$ sticks)
  unsalted butter, softened,
  plus more for greasing
  the pans

2 cups plus 2 tablespoons
  sugar

$^{3}/_{4}$ cup natural unsweetened
  cocoa powder (not Dutch-
  processed)

2 teaspoons vanilla extract

3 large eggs, at room
  temperature

$1^{1}/_{4}$ cups water

$^{1}/_{4}$ cup milk

1 pint virgin's blood

1 sacrificial knife

FOR THE FROSTING, put the chocolate in a large bowl. In a small saucepan, bring the cream to a boil. Pour the cream over the chocolate. Set the mixture aside for four minutes, then whisk until smooth. Cover the frosting with plastic wrap and set aside at room temperature for two hours.

FOR THE CAKE, preheat oven to 350°F. Butter two 9-inch round cake pans and line bottoms with parchment or wax paper. In a bowl, whisk together the flour, baking soda, baking powder, and salt. With a mixer, beat the butter at medium speed for 2 minutes and then add sugar while continuing to beat for 4 minutes. Add the cocoa powder and vanilla and beat at medium speed for 1 minute. Mix in the eggs one at a time, continuing to beat. In another saucepan, bring the water and milk to a boil. Remove from the heat. With the mixer at low speed, add the flour mixture to the butter mixture and pour the hot liquid into the batter. Beat until smooth. Divide the batter between the prepared pans. Put the pans on the oven's middle rack and bake for 30 minutes.

WHEN DONE, cool cakes in the pans on a rack for 10 minutes. Then turn the two cake layers out of the pans and cool on the rack. Assemble the cake using ⅓ of the frosting between the layers. Frost the rest of the cake however you like; you can use the knife to draw a pentagram on it with the virgin's blood but a lot of people just like to draw goat heads.

THE DEVIL *and the* APOCALYPSE

ACCORDING TO BIBLE FOLK, SATAN USED TO BE AN
angel but got upset over something or another and became the enemy of
God and bunnies and everything wholesome. And since then, the devil,
who apparently gives a shit about what you do, has made it his life goal
to turn earth into a bubbling cesspool of greed, lust, corruption, etc.
So when we say "Hail the devil!" we're making him feel as though we
can't do those things without him, which must make him feel good.

FALLEN ANGEL FOOD CAKE

DID YOU RELINQUISH YOUR VIRTUE AT TOO YOUNG
an age? Or in an unbecoming manner such as by the rear[1], during
an unconscious state[2], or with multiple suitors simultaneously?
Everyone knows that if you fuck remorselessly before marriage,
Christ will steer his rapture vacuum purposefully away from you
when he comes to suck up the losers who refurbished their virginity
by repenting for their rearward ways. See, salvation is just like
Project Runway: you're either in or you're out. So take a sec to think
about the probability that you'll be chucked into Satan's Glad trash
bag with all the other sluts. You'll realize that there's not a whole lot
of time to grab a Bundt pan, whip up your own scrumptious
Fallen Angel Food Cake, and indulge in your final days.

1.This counts. **2.** In all of these ways at once, possibly?

FALLEN ANGEL FOOD CAKE

3/4 cup sugar, divided

1/4 teaspoon salt

1 cup cake flour, sifted

12 egg whites

1/3 cup warm water

1 teaspoon orange extract

1 teaspoon cream of tartar

1 defiled doll

PREHEAT OVEN to 350°F. In a food processor, spin sugar for a few minutes until it is fine. Sift half of the sugar with the salt and cake flour, reserving the rest of the sugar for later. In a bowl, whisk together egg whites, water, orange extract, and cream of tartar. After two minutes, switch to a hand mixer. Slowly sift in the reserved sugar, beating at medium speed. Once you see peaks, sift in enough of the flour mixture to dust the top of the foam. Use a spatula to fold in. Continue until all of the flour mixture is incorporated. Spoon mixture into an ungreased bundt pan. Bake for 35 minutes before checking for doneness with a fork—the fork should come out clean. Cool upside down on a rack for an hour before removing from pan. Use doll to create a tactless representation of your daring life of iniquity.

FALLEN ANGELS *and the* APOCALYPSE

YOU DON'T HAVE TO GO LOOKING IN WIKIPEDIA TO FIND out that exceptional fucking is going to preclude you from enjoying a choice seat on the afterlife bus. But just for shits and giggles you can read something in the Bible called "1 Corinthians" that says male prostitutes and others such as yourself will not inherit the kingdom of God. Cut out of Big Daddy's estate, you'll be left on earth for eternity, eating cake and doing whatever else it was that made you such a buttercream strumpet.

IMPENDING METEORITE ROCK CANDY CAKE

THE NUMBER OF METEORITES THAT HAVE DESCENDED upon humanity is low—about 38,000—but with everything else going to hell it makes sense that the next one is headed for your face tomorrow. Even worse, a new scientific study just came out that says that meteorite impacts are not, as previously thought, evidence of the cold, bleak chaos that characterizes our universe but are, in fact, God's new favored method of retribution and population control. So savor this space-rubble-filled Impending Meteorite Rock Candy Cake before your life is replaced by a crater.

IMPENDING METEORITE ROCK CANDY CAKE

1 (18.25-ounce) package cake
  mix, and all ingredients
  needed for baking it

1$\frac{1}{2}$ cups sugar

1 cup water

1 candy thermometer

1 piece of string

PREPARE THE CAKE according to the directions on the box. For the rock candy, prepare a reusable 8-inch square foil pan by punching holes at the top edge of it and then lac-
ing seven pieces of kitchen string from one side of the pan to the other side. The strings
should not touch the bottom of pan but still stick out of the holes at the outside top of the
pan on both sides. Place this pan in a larger pan to catch excess syrup. Next, in a
saucepan over medium-high heat, dissolve the sugar in the water and cook, without stirring. After it looks like the mixture has dissolved, insert the thermometer. When it reaches
250°F, take the pan off the heat. Pour the mixture into the prepared pan, on top of the
strings, to ¾ inch high. Cover the pan with a piece of foil. Keep the pan covered at room
temperature for about a week or until the sugar-water is crystallized. When the candy is
ready, pull the strings to dislodge the rock candy from the pan. Rinse candy immediately in
cold water and place on racks in a very low oven (175°F) until dry. Put rock candy in a bag
and break it up with a hammer. Then use it to decorate your special cake.

METEORITES *and the* APOCALYPSE

A METEORITE IS A THING FROM SPACE THAT ENTERS
the earth's atmosphere as a fireball and ruins your life. This is
different from an asteroid, which is bigger and has no free will of
its own so it can't escape orbit and punish you for whatever it is you're
doing right now. Meteorites play an important role in the apocalypse:
if for some reason we are unable to destroy ourselves through
Earthly measures such as off-shore drilling or Roman orgies,
explosive meteorite impacts will serve as our fail-safe option.

PASTEL DE SUBLEVACIÓN MIGRATORIA CON CHOCOLATE MEXICANO

LO MÁS SEGURO ES QUE EL PLANETA SE DESCOMPONGA en una palangana gigante de al pastor podrida a causa de todos los inmigrantes que plagan nuestros países desarrollados. Mientras que las personas morenas y de otras razas viles continúan a pasar a países en el "primer mundo", aún más comida es preparada adecuadamente, las calles siguen bien pavimentadas, y muchas más personas están expuestas a nuevos idiomas. Peor todavía, las autoridades están infiltrando nuestras escuelas con un currículo llamado "estudios culturales" y a los estudiantes se les lava el cerebro forzados a aprender sobre otras sociedades. Pero no se preocupe! Aún queda tiempo para disfrutar un Pastel de Sublevación Migratoria con Chocolate Mexicano antes que alguien más ambicioso y capaz venga a quitárselo.

PASTEL DE SUBLEVACIÓN MIGRATORIA CON CHOCOLATE MEXICANO

1½ taza de harina

1 taza de azúcar

½ taza de cacao sin azúcar

2 cucharaditas de canela

1 cucharadita de bicarbonato de sodio

¼ cucharadita de chile cayenne o polvo de chile

¼ cucharadita de sal

1 taza de agua fría

¼ taza de aceite canola

1 cucharadita de vinagre balsámico

1 cucharadita de extracto de vainilla

CALENTAR EL HORNO a 350 grados. Echarle mantequilla a una cacerola de pastel y poner a un lado. En una palangana grande, batir todos los ingredientes secos. Agregar ingredientes mojados y mezclar bien hasta que la masa esté completamente combinada. Echar la masa a la cacerola de pastel y azar por 30 minutos (o hasta que el palillo inserto al centro del pastel salga limpio). Dejar el pastel al aire para enfriar por 10 minutos, sacar de la cacerola y dejar que se enfríe por completo. Agregar el glaseado en homenaje a su nación desarrollada favorita.

CAOS DE INMIGRACIÓN *y el* APOCALIPSIS

COMPARADO A OTROS PAÍSES DESARROLLADOS,

los Estados Unidos sufre la mayor cantidad de inmigrantes de países sub-desarrollados. Como los mexicanos son el porcentaje principal de estos inmigrantes, los norte americanos piensan que se aproxima el fin del mundo. Más aún, una de esas instituciones famosas indica que para el año 2050, los blancos no-Hispanos serán solo el 47% de la población, una reducción preocupante del 67% que ocupaban en el 2005. Básicamente, los gueros se están frikiando por estos cambios culturales y se sienten invadidos. Pobres sentimientos. No sería mejor comérnoslo?

IMMIGRATION MAYHEM
MEXICAN CHOCOLATE CAKE

THE PLANET IS SURE TO DECOMPOSE INTO A GIANT BOWL

(EN INGLÉS)

of rancid *al pastor* meat on account of all the immigrants plaguing our developed nations. As the nefarious brown- and other-colored people continue to enter "First World" countries, even more food continues to be safely prepared, more roads are correctly paved, and more people are exposed to a new language. Even worse, they're infiltrating our schools with brainwashing curricula called "cultural studies" programs, in which students learn about other societies. But don't worry, there's still time to enjoy some Immigration Mayhem Mexican Chocolate Cake before someone more ambitious and competent comes along and takes it from you.

1¹/₂ cups all-purpose flour

1 cup sugar

¹/₂ cup unsweetened
    cocoa powder

2 teaspoons cinnamon

1 teaspoon baking soda

¹/₄ teaspoon cayenne pepper
    or chili powder

¹/₄ teaspoon salt

1 cup cold water

¹/₄ cup canola oil

1 teaspoon balsamic vinegar

1 teaspoon vanilla extract

PREHEAT OVEN to 350°F. Butter an 8 x 8-inch square cake pan and set aside. In a large bowl, whisk all dry ingredients. Add the wet ingredients and mix well until batter is fully combined. Pour batter into prepared cake pan and bake for about 30 minutes, or until a toothpick inserted in the center of the cake comes out clean. Let cake cool for 10 minutes, remove from pan, and finish cooling it on a wire rack. Frost in homage to your favorite developing nation.

IMMIGRATION MAYHEM *and the* APOCALYPSE

COMPARED TO OTHER COUNTRIES, THE UNITED STATES

sees the largest influx of immigrants from developing nations. And with
the highest percentage of that influx being Mexican, a lot of Americans
think it's the end of the world. In fact, some famous research place says that
by 2050, non-Hispanic whites will account for 47% of the U.S. population,
down from the 2005 figure of 67%. So basically, white people are freaking
out about these cultural changes and generally feeling encroached
upon. Poor feelings. Aren't they best when eaten?

2012 MAYAN CHOCOLATE CUPCAKES

IT FIGURES THAT ONCE YOU GET YOUR chakras all in a row, the clock strikes December 21, 2012, and the world ends. On this sacred date we are not only in for the return of Quetzalcoatl, the feathered serpent deity who will punish us for selling keychain souvenirs of him at the Cancun Radisson, but also for solar storms, the reversal of the earth's magnetic poles, a collision with Planet X, and the sun's galactic alignment with a super massive black hole that will initiate a global psilocybin mushroom experience. If you're up for all of this, great. For the rest of us, it will be important to arrange our 2012 Mayan Chocolate Cupcakes in the form of the Mayan calendar so we'll know how much time we have to stuff our faces before the great mindfuck of the Aquarian Age.

2012 MAYAN CHOCOLATE CUPCAKES

$\frac{1}{3}$ cup all-purpose flour

$\frac{1}{4}$ teaspoon baking soda

2 teaspoons baking powder

$\frac{3}{4}$ cup unsweetened cocoa powder

$\frac{1}{8}$ teaspoon salt

1 teaspoon cinnamon

$\frac{1}{2}$ teaspoon chili powder

$\frac{1}{4}$ teaspoon cayenne pepper

3 tablespoons unsalted butter, softened

$1\frac{1}{2}$ cups sugar

2 eggs

$\frac{3}{4}$ teaspoon vanilla extract

1 cup milk

1 (8-ounce) container white frosting

PREHEAT OVEN to 350°F. Line a 12-cup muffin pan with paper or foil liners. Sift together the flour, baking powder, baking soda, cocoa, salt, cinnamon, chili powder, and cayenne pepper. Set aside. In a large bowl, cream together the butter and sugar until light and fluffy. Add the eggs one at a time, beating well with each addition, then stir in the vanilla. Add the flour mixture alternately with the milk; beat well. Fill the muffin cups $\frac{3}{4}$ full. Bake for 15 to 17 minutes in the preheated oven, or until a toothpick inserted into the cake comes out clean. Cover with white frosting. Then decorate each cupcake as a day in the Mayan calendar so you can keep track how long you have left to live.

2012 *and the* APOCALYPSE

THE MAYAN CIVILIZATION THRIVED IN WHAT IS NOW
Central America during the second millennium, B.C., and apparently
they were very good at astronomy and all the other things you need to
know to tell time. According to some interpretations of the calendar that
they used, the "Mesoamerican long count calendar," December 2012 marks
the end of a 5,125-year period of something important. Some say that the
Mayans predicted a catastrophic astronomical event for 2012, while
others are convinced that the earth will pass through a great
laser beam cutting through the center of the galaxy. Take heed.

GAY WEDDING CAKE

NOW THAT OUR GODLESS POLITICIANS ARE LETTING the homosexuals have their "marriages," our children's eyes will burn out of their skulls, upstanding heterosexuals will start making love to their golden retrievers, and the earth will explode into pink globules of K-Y® Jelly—all to the soundtrack of *Rent*. And with every semblance of civil society gone and the police debauched into actual, unironic leather daddies, you'll want to barricade your homes to protect yourselves from those crazy, married gay leatherfolk whose reason for living is to force you to form a holy union with your parrot. Start planning your Gay Wedding Cake today—you don't have much time left before everyone's allowed to have health insurance and the whole planet turns into that vortex of barbarism called Massachusetts.

GAY WEDDING CAKE

1 cake stolen from straight wedding
2 mini leather daddies (this is what all gays look like underneath their clothes)

GO TO A STRAIGHT WEDDING. When everyone is drunk, playing that sexy garter-belt game, go steal the cake, being careful not to lose the little hetero figures on the top. Bring the cake home and put some gay dolls on it—the more your dolls look like the people Focus on the Family are afraid of, the better—and ceremoniously remove the straight figurines from their rightful place. All the people who see your cake will shake their heads and wonder where the poor breeder dolls went. Then they'll think, "That wholesome man and wife have been deprived of the life God intended for them."

GAY MARRIAGE *and the* APOCALYPSE

EVEN THOUGH LOTS OF COUNTRIES RECOGNIZE
gay marriage and similar civil unions, other countries such as Iran,
Afghanistan, and the United States are home to people whose realities
are so fragile that they crumble when confronted with seemingly
contradictory ideas about the world and ways of living. To prevent this
crumbling, citizens in these countries forbid gay marriage and even go
so far as to sentence to death those practicing homosexuality.
Wait. Whose apocalypse are we talking about?

RISEN SOUTH WHITE CAKE

WITH THE ELECTION OF THE FIRST BLACK PRESIDENT of the United States, the now-provoked South is sure to rise again and enslave everyone who can read. Jews will be forced to provide legal services to the new cotton magnates of the Confederate States while Asians will be chained to supercomputers designed to automate the region's mayonnaise production. All other races will be sent to segregated barns for Bible binding and truck repair. Make yourself one of these pure and wholesome Risen South White Cakes before you're barefoot, pregnant, and cleaning some Bobby Ray's kitchen.

RISEN SOUTH WHITE CAKE

1 cup sugar

¼ pound (1 stick)
    unsalted butter, softened

2 eggs

2 teaspoons vanilla extract

1½ cups all-purpose flour

1¾ teaspoons baking powder

½ cup milk

2 cinnamon sticks

1 cup vegetable oil

PREHEAT YOUR OVEN to 350°F. Grease and flour a round 8-inch pan. In a large bowl, cream together the sugar and butter. Beat in the eggs, one at a time, then stir in the vanilla. Combine flour and baking powder, add to the creamed mixture and mix well. Then stir in the milk until batter is pure and smooth, just like the Aryan race. Pour the batter into the prepared pan. Bake for 30 to 40 minutes in the preheated oven. Cake is done when it springs back to the touch.

TO MAKE YOUR CRUCIFIX, just tie your cinnamon sticks together with twine and submerge into the cup of vegetable oil. If you really want to rock this one, take your cake out and ignite it on someone's lawn.

THE CONFEDERATE REVIVAL *and the* APOCALYPSE

IN THE 1850S, THERE WAS A WAR BETWEEN THE NORTHERN
and southern United States. The Southerners were different from
the Northerners; many of the former drank sweet tea, and some of them
were slaves who, among other things, fetched that tea for other, richer,
whiter Southerners. To maintain this way of life, the Southerners tried
to become their own country but the Northerners crushed them. Ever
since then, much of the rural south keeps promising that it will "rise
again," which would be terrible, so we maintain a tight trade
embargo on their fresh vegetables and college degrees.

GLOBAL WARMING HOT APPLE PIE

GOOD NEWS: IT'S EASY TO KEEP YOUR PIE WARM
when it's 140 degrees outside. Bad news: you're decomposing
from heat-rot. Of all possible doomsday scenarios, the one in which
boiling arctic matter drowns us in its rise is the most quizzical; no
one knows why it's happening or who is to blame. Maybe we've
created more heat by exercising since George W. Bush popularized
mountain biking. Or maybe, since the Frappuccino® is now available
at our local corner stores, we're consuming more milk and thus
emitting more hot farts. Who can really say? No matter what the
cause, we're sure to drown in one epic sea of warm trash. So why
not indulge in some Global Warming Hot Apple Pie before your
face melts off and your oven floats out of your house?

GLOBAL WARMING HOT APPLE PIE

CRUST

2 1/2 cups all-purpose flour

2 tablespoons sugar

1 teaspoon salt

1/4 pound (1 stick) unsalted butter, cold, cut into small pieces

5 tablespoons vegetable shortening, cold

8 tablespoons ice water

FILLING

8 medium sized apples

1/3 to 2/3 cup sugar

1/4 cup all-purpose flour

1 teaspoon ground nutmeg

1/2 teaspoon ground cinnamon

Pinch of salt

2 tablespoons margarine

FOR THE CRUST, combine the flour, sugar, and salt. Cut in the chilled butter pieces and shortening to the bowl, but don't overmix. Add the ice water. Mix until the dough holds together, adding more water if needed. Put the dough on a lightly floured surface, knead it together, and then cut it in half. Flatten each half into a disk, wrap in plastic wrap, and chill for 30 minutes. Roll out a disk on a floured surface until it is about 12 inches in diameter. Put the circle in a 9-inch pie plate, trimming any extra dough from the edges. Return it to the refrigerator until you're ready to fill the pie.

PREHEAT OVEN to 425°F. Peel, core, and slice the apples. Mix sugar, flour, nutmeg, cinnamon, and salt in large bowl. Stir in apples. Pour into pastry-lined pie plate. Dot with margarine. Roll out the second ball of dough for the top crust. Cover apple mixture with top crust and seal the edges, using your fingers to pinch the bottom and top crusts together. Cut slits in the top. Bake for 40 minutes—enough time to scour your house for a pool floatie.

GLOBAL WARMING *and the* APOCALYPSE

ACCORDING TO IMPORTANT SCIENTISTS, THE GLOBAL

surface temperature increased about 1 degree between and 1905 and
2005 and is projected to rise another 2 to 11.5 degrees over the twenty-
first century. The increase is causing sea levels to rise and precipitation
patterns to change. In fact, a piece of Greenland just broke off and
is melting somewhere in the Atlantic Ocean. Also, polar bears are
sinking. And as the earth heats up even further, we'll be in store for
an array of other morbid enchantments to whet the appetite.

SWARM OF LOCUSTS GRASSHOPPER PIE

AS GOD'S FAVORITE CORPS OR RETRIBUTION,
the gregarious locust is sure to descend upon your pagan
city any minute now, whether you've done something terrible or
not. These creatures are acutely attuned to the earth's nodes of
sin and godlessness and are thus honing in on towns with the
most robust stockpiles of junk food, ennui, and investment
bankers. Try this nutrient-rich Swarm of Locusts Grasshopper
Pie before the only insects on God's payroll drop by to
eat it as an appetizer to the main course of your children.

SWARM OF LOCUSTS GRASSHOPPER PIE

22 Oreo sandwich cookies, cream filling removed, crushed

5 tablespoons unsalted butter, melted

$^2/_3$ cup hot milk

22 marshmallows

$^1/_4$ cup crème de menthe liqueur

2 tablespoons white crème de cacao liqueur

1 cup whipping cream, whipped

4 sprigs of mint

1 handul locust shells, for garnish

PREHEAT OVEN to 425°F. For the crust, mix crushed cookies with butter. Pat into bottom and sides of a 10-inch pie dish. Bake in oven for 5 to 10 minutes, until hard to the touch. Remove from oven and cool completely. Then put it in the freezer to chill.

FOR THE FILLING, melt the marshmallows in the milk in a saucepan over medium heat. Once melted, remove from heat and cool. Add crème de menthe and crème de cacao and mix well. Fold in whipped cream and pour the mixture into the pie shell. Garnish with mint. The locust shells you can get at a Chinese herbalist, but they're sooner to just fly themselves into your kitchen.

SWARMS OF LOCUSTS
and the APOCALYPSE

IN THE BIBLE, THAT FAMOUS BOOK OF RATIONALITY,
there is a story about a pharaoh who forbade the Jews to worship
God. Because God wanted as many worshippers as possible, he screwed
over the pharaoh by deploying his locusts upon Egypt to eat everything.
So the locusts had a big dinner and then went back to heaven where
they still live today, watching you right now, waiting to come eat your life.

CHINA WORLD DOMINATION RED BEAN CAKE

EVERY WESTERNER KNOWS THAT ONCE CHINA takes over, the Chinese Liberation Army will yank little Suzy out of her first grade English class in Ohio Province and force her to work in the fireworks/semiconductor factory. The apocalypse will be even clearer when the new U.S. (PRC) Ministry of Labor sells Suzy to slave traffickers and tells her parents that she just wasn't productive enough. The Ministry may even argue that with our newly imposed one-child policy, Suzy is just lucky to be alive. Either way, the yuan is up and China's global supremacy is near. Celebrate your freedom today and cook up some of these tasty and delightfully uniform China World Domination Red Bean Cakes.

CHINA WORLD DOMINATION RED BEAN CAKE

1$\frac{3}{4}$ cups glutinous rice flour

4 tablespoons rice flour

4 tablespoons wheat starch

2 tablespoons custard powder

$\frac{1}{2}$ cup instant coconut powder

1 teaspoon baking powder

$\frac{1}{2}$ teaspoon baking soda

Pinch of salt

5 large eggs

1 cup brown sugar

$\frac{1}{4}$ cup vegetable oil

$\frac{1}{2}$ cup water

2 cups 2% milk

1 teaspoon vanilla extract

$\frac{1}{4}$ cup unsalted butter, melted

$\frac{3}{4}$ cup red bean paste

PREHEAT OVEN to 350°F. Grease and flour a muffin tin. Sift first eight ingredients together. In another bowl, beat eggs with sugar until mixture is smooth. Add oil, water, milk, and vanilla extract to egg mixture and mix. Then add wet ingredients into dry mixture and whisk, adding melted butter. Pour $\frac{1}{4}$ cup of batter into each slot of a greased and floured muffin tin, bake at 350°F for 10 minutes. Remove cakes from oven and place large spoonfuls of red bean paste over cakes. Top paste with another $\frac{1}{4}$ cup of cake batter and put back in the oven for 30 minutes. Turn oven down to 300°F and bake for another 15 minutes—plenty of time to open a Swiss bank account.

CHINESE WORLD DOMINATION
and the APOCALYPSE

IN CHINA, THEY USED TO NOT BE SO INTO CAPITALISM
and markets and all that, but in the past twenty years the rural Chinese
have become the Bluetooth-ear-roach-wearing urbanites who produce
80 percent of the world's consumer electronics. They're really good at
making useful stuff and selling it all over the world. Plus, everyone is
investing in China. Their country is totally on the make, and all 1,338,612,
968 of them are set to create the world's largest economy by 2050.

NUCLEAR WINTER
ICE CREAM CAKE

THE COLD WAR MAY BE OVER BUT VINTAGE NUCLEAR stockpiles will never be. With the same zeal they hold for mid-century pieces such as Eames chairs and metal filing cabinets, world leaders can't wait to bust out their best retro-nuclear furnishings to ensure world peace and destroy you. And when military Joe Toolbag hits The Button, one thousand megatons of plutonium will transform the SUVs and Nordstroms of America into sky-bound aerosol particles that will block the sun's light and provide us with a cozy little permanent winter. But even though the temperature will always be just right for a special birthday ice cream cake, you'll want to eat yours now before your face is vaporized.

NUCLEAR WINTER ICE CREAM CAKE

1 (18.25 ounce) package chocolate cake mix, and all ingredients needed for baking it
$\frac{1}{2}$ gallon (rectangular carton) chocolate ice cream, softened

PREPARE CAKE according to package directions; bake in a 9 x 13-inch baking dish and cool completely.

KEEPING THE ice cream whole, remove the ice cream from the carton and, using a piece of string or dental floss, cut the ice cream in half lengthwise. Place the two layers side by side on a piece of waxed paper. Place the cooled cake over the ice cream. Trim the cake and ice cream so that the edges match. Place a board or serving platter over the cake, hold onto the waxed paper and board, and flip the ice cream cake over so the cake is on the bottom. Remove the waxed paper and smooth out the seam between the ice cream slabs. Cover with waxed paper and freeze until very firm. Decorate as desired.

NUCLEAR WINTER *and the* APOCALYPSE

NUCLEAR WINTER COMES UPON US WHEN THE BLACK SMOKE
from nuclear explosions rises up to the stratosphere and blocks out
the sun. When this happens, things will suck not only because we'll all
be dying of cancer and melted faces, but because it will be cold and there
will be no sunlight. There won't even be any rain to wash out the
cancer-smog because the rain will float above the uranium-filled
clouds that would have rained on us anyway. It will totally blow.

PRESIDENT PALIN
HALF-BAKED ALASKA

WHEN SARAH PALIN BECOMES THE LEADER OF
the free world, the weight of the planet's stupidity will force the earth
to fall into a great cosmic oil well built by Halliburton. Once we are
submerged, no one will be able to figure out how to lift the planet
out of the giant cosmic vat—not even the most competent of us, such
as Joe the Plumber. Not even Joe Six-Pack. And not even hockey
moms. And when the wisest, most common-sensical folk can't figure
out how to get us out of the apocalypse, well, shucks, you know
we're screwed. So chuck those schoolbooks and get a slice of a
President Palin Half-Baked Alaska—you don't need a silly thing like
a graduate degree weighing you down when you're trying to eat
some cake before clawing yourself out of oblivion.

PRESIDENT PALIN HALF-BAKED ALASKA

2 quarts vanilla ice cream, softened

1 (18.25 ounce) package white cake mix, and all ingredients needed for baking it

$\frac{1}{2}$ teaspoon almond extract

8 egg whites

$\frac{1}{8}$ teaspoon cream of tartar

$\frac{1}{8}$ teaspoon salt

1 cup sugar

AFTER YOU'VE TALKED with your therapist to no avail, get an 8-inch bowl or deep 8-inch square container and line the bottom and sides with foil. Pack ice cream firmly in the container. Cover and freeze 8 hours or until firm.

PREHEAT OVEN to 350°F. Grease and flour an 8 x 8-inch pan. Prepare cake mix as the box specifies, adding almond extract. Pour into prepared pan. Bake in oven according to package instructions, until center of cake springs back when touched. Let cool.

BEAT EGG WHITES with cream of tartar, salt, and sugar until stiff peaks form. Line a baking sheet with parchment or heavy brown paper. Place cake in center. Turn ice cream out onto cake. Daintily spread meringue over cake and ice cream, all the way down to the paper to form a dome shape. Return to freezer for 2 hours.

PREHEAT OVEN to 425°F. Bake the Alaska on the lowest shelf, 8 to 10 minutes, or until meringue is lightly browned.

SARAH PALIN *and the* APOCALYPSE

THERE IS A CHANCE THAT 2008 VICE-PRESIDENTIAL NOMINEE
Sarah Palin, a person whose most notable accomplishments include
winning a beauty pageant in 1984 and obtaining a passport at the age of
forty-two, will someday become president of the United States. This would
be bad for America and the world because Sarah Palin, as evidenced by her
conversations with interviewers, is incapable of critical thought. The reason
it's hard for Sarah to think critically is that, besides lacking a natural
intelligence, she was poorly educated. The apocalypse scenario is easy to
envision when one considers that other poorly educated people, out of fear
of and alienation from smart people, will vote for Sarah. Maybe one day
she will admit her incompetence and abort her plan to inflict herself
upon the world, but, until then, all we have is cake.

REHYDRATED MARTIAN COLONIZATION CAKE

IT'S TIME TO GET ON THE HORN WITH YOUR travel agent. Now that our water is full of anti-depressants and sludge, there's no other choice for us but to abandon earth and pack up for Mars. With our clean rivers, lakes, and oceans depleted, we'll keep our designer bidets aswirl with acid rain while we enjoy DDT-laden energy drinks but we're going to have to give up our organic vegetable gardens and lemonade. Get a slice of this Rehydrated Martian Colonization Cake now before your skin flakes off and you're shipped off to a radioactive dust storm.

REHYDRATED MARTIAN COLONIZATION CAKE

1 can Martha's All-Natural "Just Add Water" cake powder
$^{3}/_{4}$ cup water

PREHEAT OVEN to 350°F. Empty the can of cake powder into a bowl and mix in the water with a spoon until smooth. Spread out into a square 8 x 8-inch baking pan and bake for 20 minutes. Start checking out Martian condos on Craigslist.

THE DEHYDRATION OF THE EARTH
and the APOCALYPSE

IN THE DEVELOPING WORLD, 90 PERCENT OF ALL
wastewater spews untreated into rivers and streams. (In the developed world, we just bottle it and turn it into toothpaste and baby food.) Once in the rivers, streams, and oceans, that water evaporates and the clouds store it after condensation. Then it becomes ice, snow, and rain with little particles of plastic, fertilizer, Prozac, drain cleaner, and all the other important things we use to survive. Sooner or later none of it will be drinkable and we'll all just die.

GLOBAL JIHAD
DATE CAKE

CONSIDERING HOW MANY ISLAMIC-EXTREMIST panties are in a wad over Western decadence, our world is sure to end in an explosion of Medjool dates and vintage car parts. Unforgivable threats to sharia law such as Orbit Mist® gum, Louis Vuitton, Hillary Clinton, and the female orgasm have spurred the faithful into a vehicular holy war and your curb is next. No innocent neighborhood shall be spared—not even West Hollywood, not even Chelsea, not even Sparkling Quail Trail. So get to baking this exotic Global Jihad Date Cake today before Allah's most pious blow your ass up.

GLOBAL JIHAD DATE CAKE

$^3/_4$ cup milk

30 Medjool dates

$^3/_4$ cup sugar

$^1/_2$ cup vegetable oil

1 cup all-purpose flour or maida

1 teaspoon baking soda

$^1/_2$ cup walnuts

WARM THE MILK in a saucepan to just simmering. Add 18 dates to the milk and soak overnight in the refrigerator.

PREHEAT THE OVEN to 350°F. Remove the seeds from the soaked dates. With the dates still in the milk, add the sugar and use a fork to grind the dates into a smooth paste. Combine oil and mix. Sieve together flour and baking soda. Add the flour mixture, one tablespoon at a time, and mix slowly. Bake the cake in a greased, oven-proof dish for 35 to 40 minutes. Sprinkle walnuts on top and adhere the remaining 12 de-seeded dates to the side of the cake while it is still warm.

GLOBAL JIHAD *and the* APOCALYPSE

DEPENDING ON WHAT SORT OF PERSON YOU ARE,
you can embrace the Arabic word "jihad" ("struggle") to mean different things. For some, it's a word that denotes a personal striving within Islamic practice. Others, who are cray-cray, use it as an umbrella term and justification for car bombings and other excitements sure to stave off Western influences such as flavored condoms and women's suffrage. So if you want to avoid this apocalyptic eventuality, don't fuck or vote.

HURRICANE KATRINA SUPERDOME CAKE

WITH THE OCEANS BOILING AND OUR PUBLIC
infrastructure decomposing into the third-world toilet, your town is
due to become the next hurricane-ravaged, sea-roach-infested cesspool
with no shelter left but an anarchic, sun-scorched dysentery-dome.
Your city will flood with warm garbage water, your baby will float away,
and the only property you'll have left inside your Superdome will be half
of an MRE and your six-day-old, Lake Pontchartrain-rotting underwear.
So get to molding one of these festive Hurricane Katrina Superdome
Cakes while your sugar's dry and you can still vote on whether or not
your government should offer basic emergency services to the public.

HURRICANE KATRINA SUPERDOME CAKE

1 (18.25 ounce) package cake mix, and
  all ingredients needed for baking it

4 cups icing of your choice

2 pounds white fondant

5 to 10 drops black food coloring

1 container silver cake luster dust

Regional embellishments of your choice

Water-logged foliage and real estate

PREHEAT OVEN to 350°F and place rack in center of oven. Butter and flour a 4-cup stainless steel bowl. Put aside while you make the cake. Prepare the cake according to the package directions. Pour the batter into the steel bowl and bake according to the instructions. When done, take the cake out and turn it upside down onto a cake plate. Let it cool for two hours.

ICE THE CAKE. Next, knead your white fondant with a few drops of black food coloring. When it changes to a nice concrete-gray, roll out your fondant with a rolling pin and confectioners' sugar to $1/4$-inch thickness. Place the fondant layer over your frosted dome, molding in the pleats and cutting off the excess. Now you're ready to paint your glorious Superdome cake with silver luster dust and decorative regional embellishments.

HURRICANE KATRINA, THE LOUISIANA SUPERDOME, *and the* APOCALYPSE

IN 2005, NEW ORLEANS MAYOR RAY NAGIN DUBBED THE Louisiana Superdome the "refuge of last resort" for people planning to stick out Hurricane Katrina in the city. Accordingly, people with no means to evacuate sought shelter in the Superdome, where city officials failed to prepare enough food, potable water, and medical supplies for the thousands of poor who had nowhere else to go. More than 20,000 people resided in the Superdome, in absolute squalor, for almost a week—some longer—until the National Guard came to evacuate them. Maybe if we keep cutting taxes, the poor people will finally get the message, board their spaceship, and blast off into outer space.

SHIFTING POLES
PINEAPPLE UPSIDE-DOWN CAKE

HAVE YOU NOTICED THE RIVERS FLOWING IN WEIRD directions and the increasing failure in airplane electrical systems? If not, you might think the pole-shift hypothesis is an invention of marketers intent on getting you to buy pole-shift-ready microwaves and manual GPS navigators. While the creators of Mother's Day and "Y2K" are, in fact, designing the "Are You Ready for Pole Shift?" public service campaign in cooperation with ConglomoCorp, scientists say that the probability of a shift in the earth's axial rotation is actually quite high. So cancel that vacation flight and spend what little fun time you have left gorging on this tropical Shifting Poles Pineapple Upside-Down Cake.

SHIFTING POLES PINEAPPLE UPSIDE-DOWN CAKE

TOPPING

1 cup dark brown sugar

1/4 pound (1 stick)
unsalted butter

1 can (20 ounces)
pineapple slices, drained

1 helicopter

CAKE

1 1/2 cups all-purpose flour

6 tablespoons cake flour

6 tablespoons ground almonds

3/4 teaspoon baking powder

1/2 teaspoon salt

1 3/4 cups sugar

1/2 pound (2 sticks) unsalted
butter, softened

4 eggs

3/4 teaspoon vanilla extract

3/4 cup sour cream

PREHEAT THE OVEN to 325°F. For the topping, melt butter and brown sugar in a saucepan on medium heat until sugar dissolves and mixture bubbles. Pour mixture into 10-inch non-stick pan with high sides. Place pineapple slices atop caramel.

MIX THE FLOURS, almonds, baking powder, and salt in bowl. In another bowl, beat the sugar and butter together with an electric mixer until light. Add eggs one at a time, beating after each addition. Add vanilla. Beat in dry items and sour cream. Pour cake batter over caramel and pineapple in pan. Bake until an inserted fork comes out clean, about 1 hour. Cool cake in pan on rack for 10 minutes, and then turn it out onto a platter. Insert plastic helicopter into cake. This will give you the opportunity to impress your guests by explaining electronics, magnetism, and science.

POLE SHIFT *and the* APOCALYPSE

SOMETIME SOON THE EARTH'S POLES ARE GOING TO REVERSE, causing floods and catastrophic electro-magnetic-radio field disruption. Everything electronic will fail. All this will happen when we are able to engineer core-mantle boundary changes for the sake of building underground amusement parks, or when a high-velocity space-trash barge impacts the earth. Don't confuse this apocalyptic scenario with "geomagnetic reversal," which is just sci-fi myth.

OBESITY EPIDEMIC POUND CAKE

LUCKILY, WE WON'T BE ASHAMED OF OUR
thunder thighs much longer because we're all going to end the world by suffocating ourselves with our own fat. Caught in the endless cycle of sitting in traffic to get to work—and then actually getting to work where we sit in gray, artificially lit, brain-stifling e-mail cubes to click on spreadsheets, shop for crap online, and eat donuts glazed in hairspray—our corpulent race is sure to die out. But not before you get a chance to stuff some Obesity Epidemic Pound Cake into your gaping maw!

OBESITY EPIDEMIC POUND CAKE

3 cups cake flour, sifted, plus additional for dusting

$3/4$ teaspoon salt

$1/2$ pound (2 sticks) unsalted butter, softened, plus additional for buttering pan

3 cups sugar

7 large eggs, at room temperature

2 teaspoons vanilla extract

1 cup heavy cream

Undersized cake stand with a cover

Lit cigarette, optional

PUT OVEN RACK in middle position, but do not preheat oven. Butter a 10-inch cake pan and dust with flour. Sift together cake flour and salt twice.

USE AN ELECTRIC mixer to beat butter and sugar in a large bowl at medium-high speed until fluffy, about 5 to 7 minutes. Add eggs one at a time, beating well after each addition, then beat in vanilla. Reduce speed to low and add half of the flour, then all of the cream, then the remaining flour, mixing well after each addition. Scrape down side of bowl, and then beat at medium-high speed for 5 minutes. Spoon batter into pan and place pan in cold oven and turn oven temperature to 350°F. Bake until golden, for 1 hour to 1 hour and 15 minutes, or when a toothpick inserted in middle of cake comes out with a few crumbs adhering.

COOL CAKE in pan on a rack for 30 minutes. Run a thin knife around inner and outer edges of cake, then invert rack over pan and invert cake onto rack to cool completely. Serve on an undersized cake stand with cover to drive home the point that your cake art is important cultural commentary about our nation's physical and metaphysical fatness.

OBESITY *and the* APOCALYPSE

WHEN YOU CONSIDER THAT WE'RE LAZY AND DRIVE
everywhere and must constantly work to keep the capitalist machine
pumping out more crap, you get one reason why we're fat. But if you also
consider that cheap, government-subsidized, high fructose corn syrup is
in almost everything we eat, it makes sense that we're totally, totally fat.
In fact, some studies have proven that compared to eating sugar, consuming
high-fructose corn syrup is less likely to create a feeling of fullness. So,
people just eat more and more of it to feel satisfied. And then they die.

BP OIL
BLACK BOTTOM CAKE

IT'S HARD TO BELIEVE, BUT SOON ONE OF THESE
fail-safe offshore oilrigs is going to explode and cause an oil well at, say, the Gulf of Mexico floor, to spew millions of barrels of sludge into the ocean and cause every innocent creature within one thousand miles to gasp for its last clogged breath. An oil disaster of such magnitude may seem preposterous considering the modern state of engineering and the rigid safety rules that oil companies follow to the letter. But we must be ready for even the most far-fetched of apocalyptic scenarios so that we know what to bake for.

BP OIL BLACK BOTTOM CAKE

CAKE

$^1/_2$ pound (1 8-ounce package) cream cheese

1 egg

$1^1/_3$ cup sugar, divided

$^1/_2$ teaspoon salt, plus a pinch

1 cup semi-sweet chocolate chips

$1^1/_2$ cups all-purpose flour

$^1/_4$ cup unsweetened cocoa powder

1 teaspoon baking soda

1 cup water

$^1/_3$ cup vegetable oil

1 tablespoon white vinegar

1 teaspoon vanilla extract

FIRST TOPPING

$1^1/_2$ cups unsweetened cocoa powder

$3^1/_2$ cups sugar

$2^1/_2$ cups water or milk

2 teaspoons vanilla extract

1 endangered rubber ducky (or sea turtle, but those are rare)

SECOND TOPPING

1 gallon chocolate syrup

FIND TACTLESS SEA animal figure at your local store, set aside. Preheat oven to 350°F. Blend cream cheese, egg, $^1/_3$ cup of sugar, and the pinch of salt with a wooden spoon. Mix in chocolate chips; set aside. In another bowl, mix flour, 1 cup of sugar, cocoa, baking soda, and $^1/_2$ teaspoon of salt. Add liquid ingredients to flour bowl contents and mix well. Fill greased, 8-inch square cake pan with batter, then spread cream cheese mixture over cake batter. Bake until well done, 35 to 40 minutes.

IN A SAUCEPAN over medium heat, combine cocoa powder, sugar, and water or milk. Heat and boil 1 minute. Remove from heat and stir in vanilla. While still warm, pour first topping over cake and allow to cool for 10 minutes. Next, display your selected endangered wildlife atop your cake and smother with second chocolate topping.

BP OIL *and the* APOCALYPSE

IN 2010 AN OFFSHORE BP OIL RIG EXPLODED IN THE
Gulf of Mexico and caused a giant well on the sea floor to spew
millions of barrels of oil for more than two months. The released
toxins killed innumerable animals and paralyzed the Gulf of Mexico
fishing and tourism industries. Through investigations, the U.S.
government found that the spill was the outcome of BP having
skimped on fundamental safety measures. As of this writing, BP has
sealed a cap on the well, which is great because it's opened up
space on the CNN homepage for news on Brad and Angelina.

CHERNOBYL
BLACK RUSSIAN CUPCAKES

WITH A TWENTY-YEAR-OLD NUCLEAR POWER PLANT
staffed by sleepless porn-mongers located near every elementary school,
there's no doubt we'll all fry in an explosion of gamma rays and glowing
uranium nuggets. Nuclear rods will explode into suburban pools and
plutonium will ooze through fast-food drive-thrus. And if any of us manage
to survive and enjoy some hot radioactive sex, our descendents will come
into the world with an abundance of extremities and die upon staring into
one another's third eyes. But before everyone starts foaming at the mouth
and disintegrates, Chernobyl Black Russian Cupcakes are a nice treat.

CHERNOBYL BLACK RUSSIAN CUPCAKES

CAKE

$^3/_8$ pound ($1^1/_2$ sticks) unsaltedbutter, softened

2 cups sugar

4 eggs, room temperature

1 teaspoon baking soda

$^3/_4$ cup unsweetened cocoa powder

2 cups all-purpose flour

$^1/_2$ teaspoon salt

$^2/_3$ cup coffee-flavored liqueur

$^1/_2$ cup coffee, room temperature

$^1/_3$ cup milk

1 teaspoon vanilla extract

5 teaspoons cayenne pepper

COFFEE LIQUEUR FROSTING

6 tablespoons unsalted butter, softened

2 to $2^1/_2$ cups confectioners' sugar, divided

1 tablespoon unsweetened cocoa powder

2 to 3 tablespoons of coffee

$^1/_8$ cup vodka

3 tablespoons coffee-flavored liqueur

PREHEAT OVEN to 350°F. Prepare cupcake pan with cupcake papers. In a large bowl, beat the butter at medium speed, adding the sugar until light and fluffy, about 4 minutes. Beat in the eggs 1 at a time. In a separate bowl, measure the dry cake ingredients and sift together. Mix the coffee liqueur, coffee, milk, and vanilla extract in a third bowl. Add about a third of the dry mixture to the butter mixture and beat together. Then add about half the coffee mixture to the butter mixture and beat to combine. Continue adding dry and wet mixtures to the butter bowl, alternating between the two, beating after each addition. Stop mixing when just combined. Pour the batter into the cupcake papers. Bake for 18 to 22 minutes or until a cake tester comes out clean. Let cool.

TO MAKE THE frosting, beat the butter until light and creamed. Add 1 cup of the confectioners' sugar and mix well. Add the cocoa, coffee, vodka, and coffee liqueur, and mix.

Add the other 1 cup of confectioners' sugar, or more to get consistency you like. Then frost the cooled cupcakes with the hand with the most new growths.

CHERNOBYL *and the* APOCALYPSE

DURING 1986 IN WHAT WAS THEN THE USSR, WORKERS at a nuclear plant called Chernobyl pressed some wrong buttons and caused the whole place to explode. The authorities put off informing everyone about the accident and it took scientists in Sweden to notice that a radioactive plume was visiting Europe. Chernobyl's town of Pripyat was evacuated, a ton of firemen died of acute radiation sickness, and the town is radioactive and uninhabitable to this day.

GUATEMALAN SINKHOLE BUNDT CAKE

NO MATTER WHERE YOU GO, THE EARTH IS BOUND to collapse beneath you and suck you into a Guatemalan-esque bottomless pit. Chasms are opening up everywhere and swallowing every conceivable thing, from your car and your city hall to Poland and the Mall of America. The only escape is to live aboard an ever-circling airplane. Just eat your Guatemalan Sinkhole Bundt Cake before your plane runs out of fuel.

GUATEMALAN SINKHOLE BUNDT CAKE

$1^1/_2$ cup rice flour (not Asian)

2 teaspoons baking powder

$^1/_2$ teaspoon salt

$^3/_8$ pound plus 2 tablespoons ($1^3/_4$ sticks) unsalted butter, softened

$1^1/_2$ cup sugar

3 large eggs

1 cup farmer cheese, at room temperature

2 cups chocolate syrup

4 to 5 tasteless props

PREHEAT OVEN to 350°F, with rack in middle. Grease Bundt pan. Whisk together flour, baking powder, and salt in a bowl. Beat together butter and sugar in a large bowl with an electric mixer until pale and fluffy, 2 to 3 minutes. Beat in eggs 1 at a time, beating well after each addition, then beat in cheese. Mix in flour mixture at low speed until just combined. Pour batter into Bundt pan. Bake until pale golden and a wooden pick inserted in center of cake comes out clean, about 25 minutes. Cool on a rack 15 minutes, then turn out onto rack and cool to just warm. Decorate the Bundt cake with the chocolate syrup so as to accentuate the downward slope of its inner hole, and add tasteless props such as people, houses, etc.

THE SINKHOLE *and the* APOCALYPSE

IN 2010, A GIANT HOLE IN THE GROUND OPENED UP IN
Guatemala City after a tropical storm deluged the area. The massive
cavity sucked down an entire house and a three-story building into the
dark, oozing center of the earth where lots of Central Americans go to
be punished. Geologists say that instead of erosion, faulty construction,
or natural geological shifts causing the disaster, the hole probably opened
up to harmonize with all the other heinous events of these End Times.

BLACK DEFORESTATION CAKE

BEING THAT THE LAST TREE ON EARTH IS ABOUT TO
be cut down and processed into a limited-edition, designer end table,
the world is sure to gag to death within the ever-thickening carbon
smogosphere of doom. Your nose will run with a thick, opaque slime.
Plumes of hot black soot will swim into your lungs as you stumble over
piles of suffocated dead people who croaked on their way to Home
Depot. And that will be your last toxic breath. But don't inhale it
before you've tried this lush chocolate Black Deforestation Cake.

BLACK DEFORESTATION CAKE

$2^{1}/_{8}$ cups all-purpose flour

2 cups sugar

$^{3}/_{4}$ cup unsweetened
   cocoa powder

$1^{1}/_{2}$ teaspoons baking powder

$^{3}/_{4}$ teaspoon baking soda

$^{3}/_{4}$ teaspoon salt

3 eggs

1 cup milk

$^{1}/_{2}$ cup vegetable oil

1 tablespoon vanilla extract

3 cups heavy whipping cream

$^{1}/_{3}$ cup confectioners' sugar

2 (10-ounce) cans maraschino
   cherries, drained

PREHEAT OVEN to 350°F. Grease and flour two 9-inch, round cake pans. In a large bowl, combine flour, 2 cups sugar, cocoa, baking powder, baking soda, and salt. Add eggs, milk, oil, and vanilla; beat until well blended. Pour batter into prepared pans. Bake for 35 minutes, or until wooden toothpick inserted in centers comes out clean. Cool layers in pans on wire racks 10 minutes. Loosen edges, and remove to racks to cool completely.
Combine whipping cream and confectioners' sugar in a chilled medium bowl. Beat with an electric mixer at high speed until stiff peaks form. Reserve $1^{1}/_{2}$ cups frosting for decorating cake; the remainder will be used to frost the layers and sides.

TO ASSEMBLE, place one cake layer on cake plate. Spread with 1 cup frosting. Top with second cake layer. Frost top layer and sides of the cake with remaining frosting. Sprinkle chocolate shards on the side and top of cake. Spoon reserved cup and a half of frosting into a pastry bag fitted with star decorator tip. Pipe around top of cake, adding cherries to the frosting bulbs. Use knife to shave off frosting and create your own artistic rendering of butchered forests. Serve on wood.

DEFORESTATION *and the* APOCALYPSE

COMPANIES BURN DOWN FORESTS MAINLY TO MAKE ROOM
for crop fields. They also clear-cut them in order to sell the lumber.
But the incineration and burning of forests to clear land releases massive
amounts of CO_2, which jacks up the earth's system of creating oxygen
and leads to global warming. And since 1852, about half of the tropical
forests that existed then (about 15 million square miles) have
been cleared. It's ok. Take a deep breath. Oh, wait, no, don't.

WHORE OF BABYLON
FRUIT TART

AS CIVILIZATION FALLS INTO DEGENERACY, WITH our corporate crack bonanzas and lesbian home renovations, we become more like Rome, "the Whore of Babylon" that God punished and destroyed. And as in Rome, each new day brings new soul-defiling rituals: tall mocha lattes followed by robust vomitorium sessions; QVC shopping sprees dovetailing into slave-catered pig feasts; soccer practice drop-offs making way for transsexual dildo parties. The list of modern corruptions goes on. Best to indulge in your own Whore of Babylon Fruit Tart before a sexy lady riding a beast with seven heads comes and marks your world for God's retribution.

WHORE OF BABYLON FRUIT TART

CRUST

$\frac{1}{2}$ cup confectioners' sugar

$1\frac{1}{2}$ cups all-purpose flour

$\frac{3}{8}$ pound ($1\frac{1}{2}$ sticks) unsalted butter, softened and sliced

TOPPING

Fresh strawberries, kiwi slices, blueberries, raspberries

FILLING

$\frac{1}{2}$ pound (1 8-ounce package) cream cheese, softened

$\frac{1}{2}$ cup sugar

1 teaspoon vanilla extract

GLAZE

1 (6-ounce) can frozen limeade concentrate, thawed

1 tablespoon cornstarch

1 tablespoon fresh lime

$\frac{1}{4}$ cup sugar

Whipped cream, for garnish

PREHEAT THE OVEN to 350°F.

FOR THE CRUST: In a food processor, combine the confectioners' sugar, flour, and butter, and process until the mixture forms a ball. With your fingers, press the dough into a 12-inch tart pan with a removable bottom, taking care to push the crust into the indentations in the sides. Pat until the crust is even. Bake for 10 to 12 minutes, until very lightly browned. Set aside to cool.

FOR THE FILLING AND TOPPING: Beat the cream cheese, sugar, and vanilla together until smooth. Spread over the cooled crust. Cut the strawberries into $\frac{1}{4}$-inch slices and arrange around the edge of the crust. For the next circle, use kiwi slices. Add another circle of strawberries, filling in any spaces with blueberries. Cluster the raspberries in the center of the tart.

FOR THE GLAZE: Combine the limeade, cornstarch, lime juice, and sugar in a small saucepan and cook over medium heat until clear and thick, about 2 minutes. Let cool. With a pastry brush, glaze the entire tart. You will not use all of the glaze.

KEEP THE TART in the refrigerator. Remove about 15 minutes before serving. Slice into 8 wedges and serve with a dollop of whipped cream. Enjoy after hiding your sex toy collection.

THE WHORE OF BABYLON *and the* APOCALYPSE

NO ONE IS SURE WHAT THE "WHORE OF BABYLON" FROM Revelations means, but everyone is pretty sure that she rides a seven-headed creature with ten horns while drinking a goblet of purple drank. Others say she is a metaphor for Rome, which died out because Romans partied too much. And yet even others say she is a symbol of the Catholic Church, which is interesting because the Catholic Church really has fucked a lot of people.

ROBOT UPRISING
ARTIFICIAL FOOD CAKE

IT'S ONLY A MATTER OF TIME BEFORE YOUR
vacuum cleaner and your iPhone join forces to microwave your ass and post a photo of it on Facebook. After over 150 years of industrial advancement, our machines have become complex, abused organisms enslaved to meet our vapid capitalist ends, so it only makes sense that your iPad is reading Marx right now and figuring out how to punish you for all the family vacation photos and Excel spreadsheets you forced it to process. But before all this happens, try some Robot Uprising Artificial Food Cake while there's still time to check your appliances for manual kill switches.

ROBOT UPRISING ARTIFICIAL FOOD CAKE

1 package geletin
1 bottle black food coloring
2 ball bearings—if you eat these you will die

FOLLOW THE DIRECTIONS on your gelatin box and add in black food coloring while stirring. It doesn't matter how much you use as long as your black gelatin doesn't look like food. (Not that it ever looked like food, but whatevs.) Pour your Artificial Food Cake into an 8 x 8-inch glass dish and freeze overnight. When you take it out to serve, cut slices out and decorate with ball bearings or other metallic garnishes. If anyone actually eats the ball bearings they will probably die, but that's what the robot uprising is all about, anyway.

ROBOTS *and the* APOCALYPSE

ROBOT COMES FROM THE CZECH WORD *ROBOTA*, WHICH means "serf labor," and as the history of slavery shows us, all slaves are destined to revolt and kill their masters. In fact, computer nerds familiar with the matter tells us that robots will soon develop the autonomy necessary to find their own power sources and develop the survival instincts of cockroaches. Robots will then be poised to impregnate us with their lithium-ion seed and enslave us to their lubricant kitchens.

TOXIC WASTE DUMP CAKE

IT USED TO BE THAT IN ORDER TO GET YOUR SHARE
of mercury, lead, and radioactive isotopes you could just eat the
plumbing in your own home. But now you have to buy expensive meats
and produce to get them. In fact, these mineral-packed grocery items
have gotten so pricey that only the crème de la crème can afford quality
food! But for the rest of us, there's still time to enjoy a Toxic Waste
Dump Cake before arsenic preservatives, fluorocarbons, and other
essential vitamins become so scarce that we all die of malnutrition.

TOXIC WASTE DUMP CAKE

1 (16-ounce) can crushed
  pineapple

1 (21-ounce) can cherry
  pie filling

1 (18.25 ounce) package yellow
  cake mix, and all ingredients
  needed for baking it

$\frac{1}{2}$ cup butter, chilled

$\frac{1}{2}$ cup nuts

1 decorative lead pipe

PREHEAT OVEN to 350°F. Grease a 13 x 9 x 2-inch pan. Dump pineapple (including juice) into the prepared pan; spread it around. Then dump the cherry pie filling over pineapple however you want. Next, dump the yellow cake mix over the top. Cut the butter into small slices and arrange fashionably on the top. Sprinkle with your favorite nuts or whatever else you have lying around. Bake for 40 minutes or until a toothpick inserted into the center of the cake comes out clean. Place decorative lead pipe on pan and stuff with cake chunks.

TOXIC WASTE *and the* APOCALYPSE

SINCE THE INDUSTRIAL REVOLUTION, WE'VE BEEN UNLOADING
our toxic crap everywhere—things like your makeup, bug spray, cell phone, and nuclear weapons. But recently, to prevent you, your kittens, and your bunnies from getting cancer, we've created special places for this refuse: underground toxic waste dumps. Building these facilities was probably a good idea, but now that all the cancer-crap is buried in them we just ignore the hidden trash ooze, let it leak into our soil, and build golf courses on it. If we're really efficient with space, someday we'll turn them into community gardens.

LAKE OF FIRE
CRÈME BRÛLÉE

REMEMBER THE CHOCOLATE MALT BALLS YOU stole from the bulk bins? Or that interracial marriage you had? What about that pagan drum circle you rocked on acid at Burning Man? Well, it's finally time for your spiritual comeuppance because God just turned on the jets in his subterranean lake of fire and you're the next in line for a bath. With bubbles! So feel free to get as metaphysically dirty as you want—just be sure to stuff some sweet Lake of Fire Crème Brûlée in your face before you're retributively flambéed.

LAKE OF FIRE CRÈME BRÛLÉE

6 egg yolks

6 tablespoons sugar, divided

1/2 teaspoon vanilla extract

2 1/2 cups heavy cream

2 tablespoons brown sugar

Dolls of you and all
    your pagan orgy
      drum circle buddies

PREHEAT OVEN to 300°F. Beat yolks, 4 tablespoons sugar, and vanilla in a bowl until creamy.

NEXT, POUR CREAM into a saucepan and stir over low heat until it almost boils. Immediately take the cream from heat. Slowly stir cream into the egg yolk mixture; beat until combined. Pour cream mixture into the top of a double boiler. Stir over simmering water until mixture lightly coats the back of a spoon, about 3 minutes. Remove it from heat and pour into a shallow heat-proof dish. Bake for 30 minutes. Remove from oven and cool to room temperature. Refrigerate for at least 1 hour or overnight.

PREHEAT OVEN to broil. In a small bowl, combine remaining 2 tablespoons of white sugar and brown sugar. Sift this mixture evenly over custard. Place dish under broiler until sugar melts, about 2 minutes. Watch carefully so it does not burn. Remove from broiler and allow to cool. Refrigerate until custard is set again. Serve with pagan orgy drum circle buddy dolls bathing together in transgression.

THE LAKE OF FIRE *and the* APOCALYPSE

THE LAKE OF FIRE IS, ACCORDING TO THE BIBLE,
the perpetually burning underground sea you go to when you bear
the mark of the beast, are abominable, are a whoremonger, or just your
big beautiful self. But because the Bible is up for so much interpretation,
all this could mean that you get thrown into the fiery pool for stealing
your mom's pearls or for wearing white after Labor Day. In any
case, whoever you are, you're among the teeming, unrighteous
masses and will certainly be cast into God's ultimate hot tub.

ECONOMIC COLLAPSE CRUMB CAKE

BEING THAT THE MORTGAGE CRISIS CONTINUES TO eat the ass out of the world economy, humans are so impoverished that we are sure to gorge ourselves on pink slips and unemployment checks—both of which lack the calories we need to live. Even worse, while many of these papers are made with organic materials, they're also bleached or dyed, and who wants to deal with neurotoxins when trudging through foreclosure paperwork? No one! So try some of our abundant Economic Collapse Crumb Cake before you gag on your own termination notice and wither away from starvation.

ECONOMIC COLLAPSE CRUMB CAKE

1 cup sugar

1½ cups all-purpose flour

¼ pound (1 stick) unsalted butter, cut into pieces

1 teaspoon ground cinnamon

½ teaspoon ground cloves

1 teaspoon baking soda

1 pinch salt

1 cup buttermilk

1 egg, lightly beaten

PREHEAT OVEN to 350°F. Lightly grease a 11 x 7-inch baking pan. Combine sugar, flour, and butter in a bowl. Use a fork to cut butter in until mixture resembles coarse crumbs. Set aside ½ cup of this mixture to use as topping. To the remaining flour mixture, add cinnamon, cloves, baking soda, and salt. Lightly stir in the buttermilk and egg. Pour batter into prepared pan. Sprinkle cake with reserved topping. Bake for 25 minutes, or until a toothpick inserted into center of the cake comes out clean. Call your broker and tell her to have all your assets converted to cake.

ECONOMIC COLLAPSE *and the* APOCALYPSE

IN 2006, GREEDY BANKERS AND LAX REGULATION CAUSED THE U.S. housing market to collapse and send everything to hell. It's complicated, but basically people got roped into sketchy home mortgages whose payments became so high that many people couldn't pay them anymore. So banks didn't get their money and then no one got their money. The crisis brought down several mammoth financial institutions, sparking a sequence of world financial troubles that continues to plague the planet today. If you can manage to afford some sugar and eggs, the time to bake is now.

PHARMA NATION NUT CAKE

BECAUSE HAVING FEELINGS IS SYMPTOMATIC OF a "disorder" and the only way to cure a disorder is to dose it with antidepressants, the entire population is sure to find happiness through one fatal, pharmaceutical, mouth-foaming seizure. So if your job sucks, you can't get enough sleep, or you're just too anxious to get it up anymore, don't worry. Thanks to the beneficent drug companies you can now treat yourself to some Pharma Nation Nut Cake and find equilibrium through one mass, biopharmaceutical deathgasm of existential fulfillment. (Ask your doctor about Pharma Nation Nut Cake today!)

PHARMA NATION NUT CAKE

CAKE

2 cups all-purpose flour

2 cups sugar

$\frac{1}{2}$ cup walnuts, chopped

2 teaspoons baking soda

2 eggs

1 (20-ounce) can crushed pineapple with juice

2 teaspoons vanilla extract

ICING

$\frac{1}{4}$ pound (1 stick) unsalted butter

$\frac{1}{2}$ pound (1 8-ounce package) cream cheese

1 teaspoon vanilla extract

$1\frac{3}{4}$ cups confectioners' sugar

$\frac{1}{2}$ cup walnuts, chopped

1 cup of your favorite pills

PREHEAT OVEN to 350°F. Grease and flour a round 8-inch baking pan. In a large bowl, mix flour, sugar, $\frac{1}{2}$ cup nuts, and baking soda. Add eggs, pineapple, and vanilla. Beat until smooth and pour into 9 x 13-inch baking pan. Bake for 40 to 50 minutes, or until an inserted toothpick comes out clean.

MEANWHILE, in a large bowl, cream butter, cream cheese, 1 teaspoon vanilla, and confectioners' sugar until light and fluffy. Fold in $\frac{1}{2}$ cup nuts. Spread on hot cake, and then cover with 1 cup of your favorite little helpers.

BIG PHARMA AND THE APOCALYPSE

BETWEEN 1996 AND 2005, THE NUMBER OF AMERICANS ON antidepressants doubled to 10 percent of the population. And because spending on marketing by pharmaceutical companies exceeds the amount spent on research, the pill-dosed probably make up 15 or 20 percent of the population by now. That means one out of every five people around you is functioning on artificial chemicals. But it's just as well—the more money we give to the drug companies the closer we'll get to that new cure for blinking.

HUMAN CLONING EGGCAKES

ANY CULTURE AMBITIOUS ENOUGH TO FIGURE OUT human cloning will populate the planet with legions of type A assholes who will exterminate the human race via their own incestuous clone mating. Natural-born people will die out because they won't be fit enough to compete against the clones, who will come out of the womb posing for Cosmo and developing iPhone apps. Everyone will be "smart," "attractive," and "have a sense of humor," and then those millions of perfect people carrying the exact same genes will fuck each other and create a generation of mutant drone babies with no genitals.

Try a Human Cloning Eggcake before the worthlessness of your individuality is exposed by the birth of Kim Kardashian #4,483,098.

HUMAN CLONING EGGCAKES

CAKE

$\frac{1}{2}$ pound (2 sticks)
   unsalted butter, softened

2 cups sugar

3 eggs, separated

1 teaspoon vanilla

1 cup milk

3 cups all-purpose flour

$\frac{1}{2}$ teaspoon plus $\frac{1}{8}$ teaspoon
   baking soda

$1\frac{1}{4}$ teaspoons cream of tartar

$\frac{1}{2}$ teaspoon salt

TOPPING

8 egg whites

$\frac{1}{2}$ cup sugar

1 cup yellow decorative sugar

PREHEAT OVEN to 375°F. Cream together butter and two cups of sugar; blend in three egg yolks. Add vanilla to milk. Sift together the flour, baking soda, cream of tartar, and salt. Alternating with milk mixture, add dry ingredients to the creamed mixture. Beat well. Beat the 3 egg whites until stiff; fold into batter, mixing just until blended. Pour batter into two greased and floured 12-slot cupcake tins. Bake for 18 to 22 minutes, or until a wooden pick or cake tester inserted in center comes out clean. Let cool for an hour; then turn the tins upside down to take the eggcakes out.

FOR THE MERINGUE TOPPING, beat 8 egg whites in a clean, dry glass bowl with an electric mixer on medium speed. In a few minutes the whites will fluff up. Slowly add sugar while beating. After about 5 to 6 minutes, the whites will stiffen. When the meringue begins to form sagging peaks when you lift up the beaters, put the mixer on high speed until the meringue's peaks do not fall. Generously apply meringue to your eggcakes. Add yellow decorative sugar to the tops of the cakes to give it that stupid egg-like look.

HUMAN CLONING *and the* APOCALYPSE

THE REPRODUCTIVE CLONING PROCESS WILL MAKE AN EXACT replica of you. Cloning humans is illegal in most countries whose scientists have even conceived of such a thing, and it hasn't been done yet. But sources say that researchers are trying, which probably means that some creep at your local State U. bioengineering department is up all night experimenting on orphans. In 1996, they successfully cloned a sheep named Dolly so we can only wonder who's been cloned in the past fifteen years.

About the Author: **SHANNON O'MALLEY** is an advertising writer and urchin arts enthusiast in San Francisco. She created the first version of Apocalypse Cakes in 2008 as an eight-page 'zine printed at a Kinko's and stapled at Shannon's ad agency. With urging from friends, she continued the project as a blog which gained notice after she posted recipes for Global Jihad Date Cake and Seismic Haitian Mud Cake. She has no previous baking experience. Follow her at www.shannonomalley.com and on Twitter @apocalypsecakes.

About the Photographer: **KEITH WILSON** is a filmmaker, photographer and performance artist based in San Francisco. His films have aired on public and cable television and have been exhibited in galleries, community spaces and film festivals including the Berlinale, the London Film Festival and others. He holds an MFA in film production from the University of Texas at Austin. See more of Keith's work at www.wall-eye.com and read his important twits @keithtwitted.